Beat Your Fear of Flying

Beat Your Fear of Flying

Captain Chris Harrison

First published 2006. Reprinted 2017
Originally published as *Beat Your Fear of Flying* by
To-Fly.co.uk

Cover design James Trigger.com
Front cover credit © Telegraph media group 2006

ISBN 978-1-5272-0544-4

Printed and bound in the UK by
York Publishing Services Ltd
64 Hallfield Road
Layerthorpe
York YO31 7ZQ

Contents

Introduction

During the next decade the number of people travelling by air is forecast to double to around three billion passengers (3,000,000,000) per year. And the pressure to travel by air will grow as grid locked traffic and overcrowded trains become the norm, because many of those road and rail journeys can be made much faster by plane – often more cheaply and with fewer frustrations.

Today, we make more journeys by air than we did ten years ago - and in ten years time we shall probably make more. But what about those of us who have a fear of flying; a fear so strong that boarding an aircraft is unthinkable? Will the limit of their world be bound by ground or sea travel while others take to the air?

Clearly pilots and cabin staff don't fear flying and will do all they can to ease the anxieties of passengers who do. For example, in the early days when the cockpit door was open, passengers were welcome to visit the flight deck. Mostly it was small children accompanied by a parent – the parent often using their children as an excuse to mask their real motive - to see the cockpit and pilots for themselves and thereby gain some reassurance.

In my experience, nine out of ten of those visitors I met admitted (when pressed) that reassurance was indeed the reason for their visit. So by showing them how safe and sturdy the aeroplane was and explaining the controls, their anxiety was quickly dispelled. Moreover they could return to their seats secure in the knowledge that the professionals flying their plane would get them to their destination safely.

That said, many of those nervous passengers had had to overcome their anxiety to take their flight originally, in spite of their fear. But what about those poor souls who find even that first tentative step too difficult to contemplate? How can they be helped?

My desire to find a solution stems from an incident that happened some years ago, when I was the Captain on a flight from Bristol UK to Palma de Majorca Spain. Some 15 minutes before departure the ground-handling agent told me that a married couple in the terminal building were struggling to board my flight. The wife, I was told, had a desperate fear of flying and was terrified to venture close to the plane. Could I help?

Well, since I'd previously helped another frightened passenger, albeit in the air, I thought it worth a try. In the terminal I found the poor lady in a terrible state, in floods of tears with her husband looking utterly dejected. Apparently they had tried to board a flight many times before, but had never succeeded.

To calm her down, I talked to her for a while, encouraging her to trust me as her pilot and suggesting that, if she wished, she and her husband could be in the cockpit for the whole flight. With gentle reassurance I coaxed her into her seat and got her to agree she would be quite okay throughout the flight. And that, I thought, should have settled the matter – but it didn't.

As I was about to leave her, she said: "Oh, just one question before we go; will you be the pilot flying us back?" I thought it best to be honest and tell her I couldn't guarantee it. However, it was quite possible she might have a much more experienced captain than me flying her back. For her, that was unacceptable and, if I couldn't give her the guarantee she wanted, she wasn't going. So she got up and walked off the aeroplane, leaving her thoroughly despondent husband to forego his longed-for holiday and follow her off.

Given more time with her I'm convinced we could have succeeded, but time was a luxury I didn't have at that time as we had a schedule to keep and delays are expensive. Since then, I have thought a lot about that incident and considered what more I could have done to dispel her anxiety - which is what prompted the years of research and understanding of the psychology of fear that has gone into this book.

The answer lies in understanding your anxiety, what drives it and the methods to mitigate that fear. Given that perspective, a flight on a plane can be treated much the same as a journey by train or car. It really is **that** simple.

You might wish to read this book in any order you like, but do read it all. I have introduced the understanding of the mechanics of flight and what the processes involved are, early on so that by the time you reach the methods on how to relax and how to cope with those anxieties you will have a greater understanding of what is happening outside of your direct control. Like Reg Hewitson on the back cover, go back over it again and again, if it helped him it should help you too.

What is a Fear of Flying?

In the beginning when man was a cave dweller, he had very little knowledge of his world, but he soon got to know what was dangerous to him and what was not, and as he learned to avoid the harmful elements, he developed the "fight or flight" mechanism, to stay and fight the beast or run to save his skin. Either way his "sympathetic nervous system" tripped in, physically putting his body on heightened alert; adrenalin pumping through his blood stream, heart rate increases, breathing rate increases, metabolism and blood pressure increases, all preparing him physically to carry out his task as hunter or getting away as quickly as possible.

There is a theory called "the Preparedness theory" which suggests we are biologically prepared to avoid such dangers instinctively, for example, lions, tigers, crocodiles etc, not that you would see many of those in the high street! Certain fears are necessary in order to live our lives safely, would we happily travel on a bus if we could see the driver was drunk? I doubt it! We can also exist in a state of fearful anxiety when there may be a threat of danger, for example a soldier about to go into battle. We have come to develop as a race a whole raft of fears and phobias from the obvious to the most obscure. It has been shown that specific phobias can be induced on purpose.

In a famous experiment conducted by psychologists Watson and Rayner, in 1920 an 11-month-old toddler called Albert was allowed to play with a rat. Naturally little Albert showed no fear, however subsequently each time Albert was introduced to the rat, a loud noise was set off behind him, which made him jump and start to cry. After several more of these episodes all poor Albert had to do was see a rat and he would burst into tears, he even developed a fear of anything that was furry; an example of classical conditioning similar to Pavlov's salivating dogs. The issue here is that little Albert started off without any fear but was taught to be fearful, so he in effect <u>learned</u> the fearful behaviour. The good news is that what can be learned can also be "unlearned". I understand the experimenters desensitised Albert, it's even possible he grew up to run a championship rat breeding business!   In other experiments with people and animals it was shown that desensitisation could remove the learned fear response, which means a learned fear, as in flying, can be equally well unlearned.

A fear of flying is a specific situational phobia. Much like any other phobia it is defined in DSM V (the diagnostic statistical manual (fifth revision) of mental disorders, as used by psychiatrists and psychologists worldwide) as.

An irrational and abnormal fear, invoked by a particular object or situation where the fear is out of proportion to the demands of that situation and cannot be explained away, it is also beyond voluntary control and leads to avoidance of the feared situation.

So now we know that a fear could relate to something that has a real potential to harm us, but a phobia is irrational and abnormal, as there is no real immediate danger involved. So maybe we should refer to fear of flying as a flying phobia. If it was rational and in proportion then why would we try to seek help in overcoming our flying phobia? Because the great majority of sufferers acknowledge that the fear symptoms they experience are irrational.

There are three stages of development of the phobia and the people affected can be split into three groups,

Group 1 are those that are able to fly; however they experience mild or moderate apprehension about the flight. They usually are the ones who have white knuckles gripping the seat in any mild turbulence.

Group 2 are those that experience considerable discomfort long before the flight and/or during the flight. They may have to resort to tranquillisers or drink excessively before and during the flight.

<u>Group 3</u> this group is unable to fly at all and avoid any situation that may bring them into contact with a possibility of flying. This group can experience a panic attack just by thinking about flying.

Does any of the above ring a bell with you? Don't worry you are not alone. Studies have shown that approximately 1 in 5 people or 20% of the population are in one of the above groups. In Great Britain alone that means 12 million people have a fear of flying or 57 million in the USA. Flying phobia is a disorder that can be treated effectively though and success rates of up to 98% have been reported. So take heart!

Well; you may recognise some of those 3 levels of fear above but I guess you would agree you weren't born feeling that way, so what happened? Some where along the way you learned to have a fear of flying. There are many ways this could have happened. You could have learned it from your parents or siblings, or you could have had a bad flight experience in the past and began to fear a repeat performance. It could be a result of stress relating to a fear of something unavoidable and so transferred that fear to something that was avoidable: flying. You could suffer from a condition whereby you have a fear of panic or even of fear itself, if you have had a succession of negative experiences that reinforce each other they can escalate to become a phobia and even transfer to other areas of life. A past trauma can attach itself to flying; for example a severe car crash on the way to the airport for a flight could then link crashing and flying together.

A fear of flying can in some cases be the presenting symptom of underlying phobias such as claustrophobia (closed in spaces), agoraphobia (crowds, open spaces), acrophobia (heights), social phobia, (engaging with other people) hydrophobia, (crossing water and oceans) and even phobophobia, (fear of shaming oneself by demonstrating fearful emotions). I have spoken to many mothers who have begun to develop a fear of flying from a feeling that if they were to die in a disaster, they would then leave their child to grow up motherless and without care and direction.

A secondary gain can sometimes be the underlying reason behind a development of fear of flying, for example, a husband who travels the world regularly on business asks his wife to join him, now for whatever reason, she does not really want to go with him, (I am sure you can think of several) so she develops a fear of flying to justify her reason for not joining him and after a period of time she starts to believe it herself.

Quite often the individual does not know where or how the phobic trigger originated, it might have been a long time ago in the past, what is useful to know is, if the phobia is related directly to flying and not to an underlying phobia like those just mentioned, whereby specific treatment of that phobia could remove the inability to fly.

Ok so now we have an idea what a phobia is, so how are the fearful flyers different from the rest of the population? It's simply how our minds work, how and what we think, and how our emotions respond to those thoughts, lets take a few examples.

Someone tells you in graphic detail about a recent meal they had at a restaurant, although you weren't thinking about food beforehand you may well start to feel hungry and even your salivary glands might start to work. You may start to think about a situation where you were badly done by and you start to feel anger rising within you. You were in a happy mood before you sat down to watch a sad film but you might well shed a tear before the end. All these are natural emotional responses to a particular train of thought. So if you are a fearful flyer, thinking about flying will make you feel anxious and you could start to feel the physical symptoms of anxiety such as sweaty palms, raised heart rate, breathing faster, feeling tense, butterflies in the stomach and worse. All those responses from a thought!

In order to know why we have those responses to our thoughts we need to know a little of how our minds work, don't worry its not rocket science and we can use analogies to simplify the process. The mind is made of two different parts,

The conscious

The subconscious or unconscious

These parts are not separate but are functions of the same mind. The conscious is what we use in the here and now, we use it to collate what we hear, see, smell, think, feel, experience; from these senses we make a perception of that event, we then compare this with our stored and accumulated database of perceptions in the subconscious and based upon that association we make an interpretation which is then used to do two things, it is used to make an evaluation of how it might affect us and on that evaluation we decide a course of action to either do something, ignore it or repress it.

The other thing that happens is, that interpretation of reality is stored within our subconscious for use next time the process is repeated. This storing or "recording" actually starts before birth and so all of our earlier recordings will affect the way we perceive things later on. These recordings also include what we think about those experiences, what we say to ourselves about them and also our emotional reactions to them.

These recordings in our subconscious are how we perceive the truth, and here is a very important point, it may well not be the absolute truth but only the truth as we see it. The subconscious doesn't make judgements; basically if we record something negatively about our abilities, surroundings or emotions then our actions will be carried out in a manner that reflects that. In effect if our picture of truth and reality is based upon misinformation then our behaviour and actions will be inappropriate. And this is an important concept in the formation of the phobia.

If way back in the past we have picked up some information about flying, a good example would be to have seen something in the media concerning an aircraft incident, it may be "recorded" as "flying looks dangerous". Without the complete understanding behind the incident, the seed of misinformation has been sown and each time that recording in our mind is revisited it will reinforce the misinformation to then become "flying is dangerous" and as such it should be avoided; reinforcing that perception until it becomes a fear and with repetition that fear becomes entrenched.

The pattern develops whereby the individual starts to worry well in advance of any planned trip and starts to become obsessive about what could happen, it's called "catastrophising"; for sure something terrible is going to happen to them. You can hear them at airports talking to one another, drawn magnetically to each other to discuss their fears and somehow to agree that they are right to feel that way. The result of perceiving themselves in a fearful situation is that the "fight or flight" mechanism trips in, as in the case of our early ancestors out hunting for food, except here inside an aeroplane they are unable to escape from the perceived danger. The brain activates the sympathetic nervous system, which prepares the body to cope with danger and starts the physical preparation, which in the case of an inability to escape can lead to a panic attack. The symptoms of which can be a few or all of the following, sweating, shortness of breath and or a smothering sensation, palpitations and accelerated heart rate, chest discomfort or pain, dizziness or faintness, nausea or abdominal distress, numbness or tingling sensations, flushes or chills, trembling or shaking, a fear that the individual is dying or at least having a heart attack or a stroke, or going crazy or about to do something out of their control.

Generally a panic attack is associated with very rapid breathing called hyperventilation and if left unchecked could lead to fainting. It is important to know that the body will recover, because if fainting occurs the anxiety provoking thought processes stop, the breathing rate will return to normal and the individual will revive in a very short time. This is obviously a very stressful situation to the individual especially if they have been in that situation before, they then begin to fear the fear itself and as the fear rises so they begin to anticipate a panic attack and so a self fulfilling situation occurs. **All this stemming from misinformation**.

So what are the emotions that make us fearful? A feeling that flying is dangerous and that we could die in a crash, we will discuss that later on and you will see how completely improbable that is. It could be a loss of control whereby we feel completely helpless to affect anything as we sit there in the aeroplane. How often do we hand over control to others in our lives? We actually do it all the time without really being aware of it, if we jump into a car as a passenger with a friend or partner driving; that is loss of control, albeit we can interact with the driver.

Another example would be in a bus or particularly a train where it is impossible to communicate with the driver. An example of totally giving up control would be if we need an operation, we give our bodies to the surgeon in complete faith of his abilities without question, as of necessity he delves within us. So why should we feel out of control in an aeroplane, could any of us do a better job than the two pilots and several autopilots in the front? All we need to do is <u>be totally in control of our own thoughts and hence emotions.</u>

Research has shown that newspapers and the TV report a significant bias towards death from violence like homicide, tornadoes, floods, terrorist attacks, vehicle accidents, drowning, etc. These are reported far more frequently than deaths from illnesses like cancer or diabetes, the fact is death by illness is 15 times more likely than death by accident. What this means is, events that seem commonplace are far less newsworthy than events that are unusual or spectacular in nature. A collection of newspapers in one period reported 528 deaths by homicide and only one by diabetes. So how does this all relate to a flying anxiety? Well people who have very little or no experience of flying, rely upon information from the media, who distort the perception of the safety elements of aviation and report any incident no matter how minor in a sensational way. Why do they do this? It's pretty obvious- to sell papers. Aviation incidents are so rare that even the smallest accident without any casualties makes headline news.

A good example of how our perception of danger can be manipulated by even the entertainment industry was the film "Jaws", if you saw that film (about a monstrous great white shark, attacking anything and everything) you would think twice about even dipping your toe in the sea, let alone going for a swim. Before that film I guess you never thought about it twice. This goes to show how a completely hypothetical film can affect people's thoughts and actions.

Ok so you may still believe that if you were to take a flight something would happen, deep down you may think it is irrational and something personal to you. So why do you believe that? Look at the statistics in the next chapter then ask yourself why me? Yes, why me? Do I have the ability to see into the future? Am I clairvoyant? Of course not so keep questioning yourself and read on.

As we have discussed, our feelings follow our thoughts, so in order to feel differently we have to **think differently**. I know that's easy for me to say but by the time you have taken in the information further on about thought stopping and changing, you may well be able to rationalise your thoughts.

One of the facets of maintaining fear and or a phobia is avoidance of the fear-provoking situation, it may well give relief in the short term as a safety seeking behaviour but it increases the anxiety in the long term.

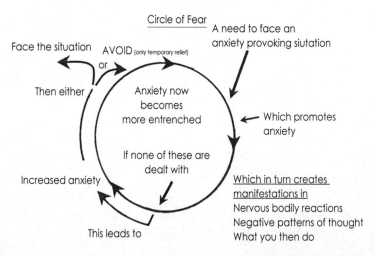

Circle of Fear

A need to face an anxiety provoking siutation

Face the situation   AVOID (only temporary relief)
or

Then either

Anxiety now becomes more entrenched

Which promotes anxiety

If none of these are dealt with

Increased anxiety

Which in turn creates manifestations in
Nervous bodily reactions
Negative patterns of thought
What you then do

This leads to

As with any fear of an object or situation we have to be a little bit courageous and face up to it. Lets take an example, say someone with a fear of spiders, even though they know that in the UK there are no poisonous ones and even if one were able to bite it would do no harm, they still have that fear, so what do they do? They avoid them. This in turn strengthens the fear of spiders, many of you who have a fear of flying but not of spiders may find that hard to understand and of course vice-versa, but the principles at work are the same. So the spider phobic has to start breaking the avoidance pattern, a good way to start is to get comfortable with being gradually closer and closer, and then maybe picking up a tiny money spider and getting comfortable with that, then slowly moving to bigger ones until its possible to be able to catch a large house spider between their hands to put it out of the house.

With each progressive stage the fear diminishes until it becomes exhausted and no longer exists. What now remains is a sensible approach to spiders in that the individual would quite rightly be wary of handling a tarantula for example unless in controlled conditions.

With each stage or progression so confidence builds and eventually the anticipatory anxiety can turn to anticipatory pleasure. I do know this process works because I used to have a fear of spiders, I had to get my wife to put them out of the house, but now I am quite happy to handle them. During all of this process of breaking the avoidance pattern, it's possible that you might experience some of the physical symptoms like sweating, heart rate up, etc so what! You won't die, it may be unpleasant but you can cope with it. It is generally agreed among the medical fraternity that the best way to overcome any fear or anxiety is to come face to face with it. In the case of flying it may not be possible through cost or opportunity to take regular flights, however imagined flights can be undertaken. By imagined I mean just imagine you are going to the airport and taking a happy successful flight somewhere, try doing this regularly, say before you go to sleep or if you have some spare time during the day. The fact that you are starting to perceive flying as uneventful, helps to establish positive patterns in the brain.

Repetitive Exposure to anxiety

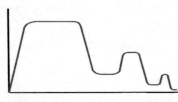

A constant exposure at repeated intervals to the object of anxiety gradually reduces that anxiety. This has been shown to be the single most effective way to eliminate an irrational anxiety or phobia.

Constant stimulus
Time Interval

How can we relate breaking the avoidance pattern to flying? It's exactly the same, find out where you want to begin, say thinking about flying, going <u>to</u> the airport, going <u>into</u> the airport, booking a flight, taking a flight; gradually build up to it until you feel comfortable and ready and let your self confidence increase with each stage. Just start by breaking that circle of avoidance.

It's odd how humans when faced with a fearful situation start to behave and think completely differently from their normal pattern, they start to think irrationally, negatively, the worst will happen to them, those that make it onto the flight become over sensitive to anything, the mind working overtime. For example a normal noise like a hydraulic motor running (but new to them) is perceived as a disastrous portent of something about to go terribly wrong. A little understanding of how the aeroplane works and knowing that there will be noises from around them would help them to cope rationally, so the chapter on the aeroplane should help here.

Another consideration that some people attribute to the development of a fear of flying is that it is unnatural, if God had meant for man to fly he'd have given him a bigger bank balance, or at least a set of wings. Although man has his physical limitations, as do all the other animals in the world, he has developed over time to be at the top of the food chain out of all the bipeds, quadrupeds, vertebrates, invertebrates and crustaceans. What made him different? Intelligence. If a set of wings would have made early man a better hunter, evolution over the aeons would have certainly engineered some for him, what happened to the pterodactyl? You don't see many of those in your garden now.

So whether an animal has wings depended upon its evolution of needs for survival, there are animals that had wings and have started off flying and eventually lost the ability to fly, for example the chicken, ostrich and dodo. It may come to pass in the far off future that man may develop wings and fly! And then it would be a perfectly natural occurrence.

Aviation is a relatively new phenomena, powered flight has been around for just over 110 years and the internal combustion engine not a lot longer than that, the laws of physics relating to flight have always been there, birds have used them all along, it has just taken man until now to discover them to use to his advantage, prior to their discovery man thought it was an impossible dream, however as we enter a new era of man flying into space for pleasure, and visiting the planets and stars as our world becomes too small, what could be more natural than the flight from one city to another.

Some Statistics

Statistics may not be a great comfort for the fearful flyer, but by knowing a few facts it certainly helps them to put their anxiety into perspective and hopefully to develop at least an understanding of the immense safety of flying. The western world has led the way in aviation development and also the culture of safety, which permeates every corner of aviation. Every aspect of aviation is being re-examined again and again, the individual and the governing bodies never let up on their quest for safety. Aviation is the most regulated, examined and scrutinised industry in the world, why? To eliminate complacency, not that it exists, to strive towards the ultimate goal of never having an accident. The man-machine interface strives to eliminate our human weaknesses of being fallible and we in turn monitor the machine because it in turn is not perfect, it has also been built by man.

Although flying is worldwide, there are indeed cultural differences from region to region and country-to-country that can have an influence on the ethos of safety, The developing countries do, it is recognised have some way to go to match the safety record of the developed world, and world statistics on flight safety also include areas such as parts of Africa, South America, China, Russia, which distort the general impeccable safety record.

We as a travelling public are interested in figures that relate to airline transport, that arena of aviation where we would be involved, not to other areas of aviation into which we may never ever venture, for example, sport flying, hot air balloons, air racing and competitions, air shows, bush flying, gliding and military aviation. Unfortunately the press reports any incidents in these areas, and we naturally log them into our subconscious to distort our perceptions of flying safety. Why do the press make such a big thing of any aviation incident? **Because they happen so rarely,** it makes for good editorial reviews, and of course it can be milked for days. Does an accident on our roads make headlines? Of course not because it is so commonplace, in fact did you know that.

Flying is 25 times safer than driving in your car.

In 2002 in the UK alone 300,000 people were victims of road accidents, and 3,400 were killed.

As you turn the ignition key in your car, do you ever consider the safety implications before you drive off? Probably not because you doubt anything will happen to you, look at the statistics above.

In 2003 there were only 27 fatal air accidents to airliners *worldwide*, with only 720 fatalities

(those mostly occurred in Africa and the developing world)
Annually 1,500,000,000 (1.5 billion) air passengers travel safely.
Source, aviation safety network

If we assume an average passenger complement per flight of 150 then there are 10,000,000 (10 million) safe aircraft flights per year.

In the UK between 1990-1999 (ten years) there were <u>no fatal accidents</u> and 706,000,000 (706 million) passengers travelled safely
Source, statistical survey by UK CAA, cap 70 aviation safety review 90-99

Finally to put this into a perspective that is relevant to us individually; If you were to take a random commercial flight every day, it would take 26,000 years before you had an accident.

Or to put it another way if you were to live to be 80 years old, you would have to live for 350 lifetimes before you had an accident.

The numbers above are staggering and too many to visualise, the odds of having an accident are so small that they pale into insignificance against say driving to the corner shop in your car. There are those who will say, " there is still an element of danger in flying no matter how small, and I just know that something will happen to me". Can we go through life without accepting a small risk in everything we do? No of course we can't or we would never get out of bed in the morning. Just about everything we do in life involves an element of risk, the odds of being struck by lightning are much higher than being involved in an aviation accident. Should we not go outside then? Accidents in the home kill more people than aviation, should we not stay inside then? What a dilemma, no of course it isn't, we have learned to accept risk as part of our everyday lives. We all want to live to a ripe old age and slip away quietly in our sleep, but at the same time we know it isn't always like that and anything could happen to change that ideal. So here is the point, we should **accept that miniscule element of risk** in flying as part of living our lives. Look upon flying differently, yes the unthinkable could happen, just as we could get struck by lightning, accept it and your fear will be greatly diminished.

The Aeroplane

For many of you the aeroplane may be the incarnation of all your fears, but by developing an understanding of how they fly and how they work will certainly help in dispelling many misconceptions and misunderstandings which can be the bedrock of a fear of flying.

The birds have mastered the theory of flight without knowing the simplest of formulae, they have been doing it since time immemorial, in fact the knowledge is inbred within their genes, the tiny fledgling jumping from the edge of the nest knows instinctively how to fly, either that or he is an incredibly fast learner! The laws of flight that enable the birds to fly are identical to those, which enable the mammoths of the sky like the 747 and Airbus 380 to fly.

The air behaves in much the same way as a fluid although we can not see it, we know its there, try putting a hand out of a car window at speed you can feel it pushing back, put moisture into it and you can see the clouds, mist or fog. It can be weighed; a column of air stretching from the surface to the edge of space weighs about 15 lbs or 7½ kgs or equivalent to a column of mercury 760mm tall, it exerts this force all around us. We can see the strength of the air when it moves at hurricane force and how it can treat solid structures like buildings as though they were made of paper.

The Wing

The early aviators studied the shape of a bird's wing and emulated it on their designs of flying machines without really understanding the aerodynamics behind it. Nature as always had it right and with the advent of wind tunnels it was possible to see using smoke, how the air flowed over a wing to develop lift. Nature doesn't like a vacuum, which is why one can't be found naturally, we can contrive to make one but again nature will fill the void and this natural force can be harnessed to develop lift.

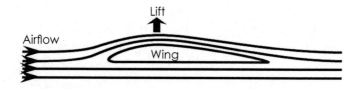

Diagram 1. Airflow travelling over the camber of a wing

In the diagram above the air is flowing from left to right over the shape of a wing, as the air right in front of the forward edge of the wing has to move up and over the wing it has further to travel in order to reach the back end at the same time as the freely moving air. In order not to create a vacuum it therefore has to travel faster over the top of the wing. Another law of physics states that the pressure and velocity of moving air remain constant: increase one then you decrease the other. In the diagram above the air is moving faster over the top of the wing so the pressure decreases, creating a tendency towards a vacuum which nature again doesn't like so it will try to exert a force upwards on the wing to reduce the vacuum, this force is called lift. The faster we move the air across the wing the more lift we can achieve. For any technical buffs: an early mathematician called Bernoulli came up with the theory that lift generated was dependant upon the size of the wing, the speed of the wing through the air and the density of the air. So in simpler terms the bigger the wing more lift is developed, so that's why a Jumbo has a big wing in order to take all that weight into the air at the same speed as a smaller aeroplane. If a jumbo was to fly at the speed of say a Concorde it would need a very small wing to achieve the same amount of lift. Runways are built to a certain length, because they are very expensive to build and can't be made longer for physical reasons, that being so aircraft have to be designed to use the average runway length. The purpose of the runway is for the aeroplane to accelerate to a speed whereby the wing can develop enough lift to get airborne, seems logical! But what happens if the runway is not long enough? Well we need to increase the size of the wing, how do we do that? We use a device called a flap, it doesn't actually flap but slides out behind the wing, following the camber shape of the wing to make it bigger, and also making the airflow over the wing go further and therefore faster, developing more lift. Many aeroplanes employ devices at the front of the wing as well.

A view of flaps in the full down (landing) position, and 2 raised (speed brakes) also called spoilers, on a   Boeing aircraft. You would normally see this configuration just after landing.

Photo author

Shortly after take off as the aircraft is accelerating away there is no more need for these devices, so they are retracted back into the wing, they are either operated by electric motors or more usually by hydraulic motors which are often located underneath where you sit, hence the loud whirring noise a few minutes after take off.

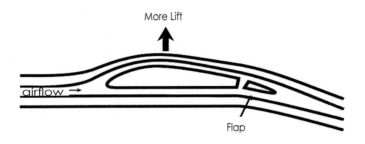

More Lift

airflow →

Flap

Diagram 2. Airflow over the wing now has further to travel due to the flap being lowered

Wheels and Brakes

In the same manner the wheels that were required for take off are now just dangling in the air creating drag, so they are also brought up into the wing or belly of the aeroplane a few seconds after take-off, again the hydraulic motors start to whirr as they retract them out of the way, quite often they make a definite clunk as they are locked into position for the rest of the flight until just before touch down. During flight the aircraft can fly at speeds of up to 500+ mph or 800+ kph, high up in the air above the clouds and birds where the air is thinner and less resistant to forward speed so we can travel faster and therefore cover longer distances for less fuel used. We now have to slow right down to land on the runway. So that we can easily and safely stop the aeroplane before the end, we use our flaps again to increase the size of the wing to enable us to safely fly slowly. The average speed for most large airliners before touchdown is anywhere between 100-180 mph or 160-228 kph, so then when on the ground the wheel brakes need to be very efficient to slow down up to 2 or 3 hundred tons of machine.

Another clever device is used to help the aeroplane to slow down and they are the speed brakes or spoilers as they are called because they "spoil" the lift over the wing, they are large boards along the centre of the wing, which are raised just after the main wheels touch the ground.
These spoilers are also used in flight If there is a requirement to slow down quickly, for example to fit in with air traffic control requirements, or entering a holding pattern where exact speed control is needed, sometimes during descent you can see them raised and they create a slight vibration which can be felt as a buzz.

Another familiar slowing technique is the use of reverse thrust, which basically through a system of linkages and doors deflects the engines thrust forwards when on the ground (this can be quite noisy). The net result of all these facilities to slow down the aeroplane means it can land on quite short runways, but don't forget it will have to take off again from the same place! So this is all considered before the landing is planned.

Fokker 70 of KLM showing reverse thrust deflection doors open at rear of engines.

It can happen sometimes that you may experience what is termed a firm landing! And you may well ask why have firm landings when the pilot could have made smooth ones? Quite often at the landing airport there may well have been a lot of rain, which is sitting as standing water on the runway, and a smooth landing on top of that could easily start the tyres to aquaplane, so that the braking could be seriously compromised. It is then necessary for the tyres to break through the depth of water to the concrete in order to spin up the wheels and make good contact. Another reason may be that there are strong crosswinds on the landing runway and just before touchdown as the aircraft is aligned into the direction of the runway, before any sideways drift can take effect and with a minimum of float the aircraft is firmly placed on the runway. Every pilot likes to make a landing that is so soft the passengers don't know they have landed, but for safety reasons that isn't always possible.

Engines

One question I am often asked is "what would happen if all the engines quit, would the aircraft fall out of the sky?" the simple answer is no of course not, all aeroplanes can glide, in fact before commencing most descents the engines are brought back to idle power which is the same as zero thrust (just like taking your foot off the accelerator in your car), the aeroplane then becomes a big but fast glider, from cruising altitude the average gliding distance is about 150 miles or 240 kms, in fact this gliding capability is part of the normal operation of a large airliner. All multi engine aircraft are designed to operate with the loss of an engine and 4 engine aeroplanes can function with 2 engines not working.

Modern engines are at the forefront of reliability and the incidences of engine shutdown are a very, very rare occurrence. The engines are tested by firing large (dead) birds into them at maximum engine speed to ensure their integrity, because bird strikes are a possibility. In over 35 years and over 16500 hours of airline operations I had only once had to shut down an engine in flight on a 4-engine aeroplane as a precautionary measure only, the rest of the flight proceeded normally, and that was almost 30 years ago on an almost 20-year old aeroplane! Things have improved beyond recognition in 50 years.

Controls

We all know what an aeroplane looks like and roughly where the wing goes, but what about all those other sticky out bits at the back? Well we need those and the "ailerons" at the ends of the wing to change direction and altitude. They are moved in response to a pilot or autopilot input through the control columns in the cockpit, these in turn either through cables to actuators, or fly-by wire, which refers to the electronic connections from the control column or side stick to the hydraulic actuators power the large control surfaces.

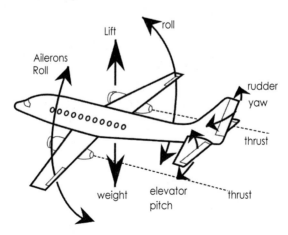

Diagram 3. Showing control surfaces and their effects.

Remember how we developed lift with the wing and increased it by lowering flaps, well we can do much more by using the same principles.

The rudder and fin are at the back and stick vertically upwards; they usually have the airline logo painted on them. They act just as a rudder in a boat to change direction, called yaw. If this was used only to control direction change it would be pretty uncomfortable and also our drinks would slide off the table! So they are used in conjunction with ailerons for roll control to make a balanced turn, quite often passengers are unaware that a turn has been made it is so gentle.

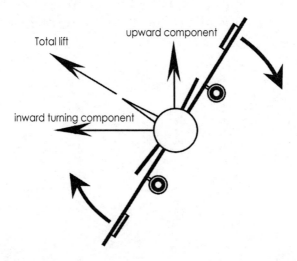

Diagram 4. Showing the components of total lift where the rolling effect has created an inward turning effect.

The ailerons are situated at the ends of the wings and as one goes up the other goes down, one produces more lift at the end of the wing and the other less lift, hence a rolling tendency. Because the wing overall produces lift upwards, this rolling of the wings angles the lift in towards the direction of roll creating a turning force.

The elevators at the rear of aeroplane do exactly that; control the elevation using the same principles as before. The aircraft weight is balanced by the lift generated at a point on the wing, and by changing the lift at the elevators, up or down, the aeroplane can be made to pitch the nose up or down pivoting around that point on the wing. In doing this, the angle of the wing to the oncoming airflow is changed, creating more lift=climb or less lift=descend.

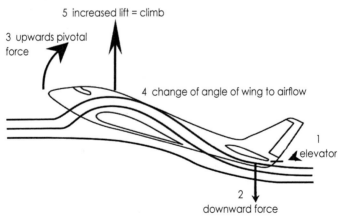

Diagram 5. Showing how elevator changes create climb and descent.

Just about all aeroplanes have a similar layout of controls from the smallest single seater to the biggest airliner, and the controls in front of the pilot work in exactly the same fashion.

It is reassuring to know that modern airliners are built with the capability of multiple redundancy, which means all critical systems like for example the flight control systems are triplicated, as are the electrical systems, pressurisation, landing gear extension, navigation, air conditioning and many of the secondary systems are duplicated even down to the position lights in the wing tips.

If you have managed to follow all that and understand it all then take a pat on the back, you deserve it. In the following chapters we will take a look at the people involved in the overall operation of the aeroplane.

Aviation People

It's perfectly natural to want to know about the people in whom you are placing your implicit trust, those people to whom you entrust your safety. I would hope you will gain reassurance about them in the following pages and that you will be able to dispel yet another possible misguided cause for concern, lets start with the people with whom you are most familiar.

The Pilots

To become a pilot is not an easy task, first one needs to have the right motivation, a lot like a vocation, one can't just find oneself offered the job as a natural promotion or to fill an empty vacancy. Most pilots knew right from when they were children that was what they wanted to do, in a way just like a doctor did. There are hurdles all along the way to finally becoming an airline pilot. They need to be academically bright, at least to a higher level of education, they have to be fit enough to pass an extremely stringent medical that seeks to determine their inner organs ability to continue functioning normally until well past retirement, their eyesight, reactions, psychological suitability, etc are all closely examined. The next big hurdle is the huge cost of training; which can take on average up to two years of intense study and practical training, many young people borrow heavily from the bank or re-mortgage their homes, then they can start with continual flying training and assessments, classroom studies and written exams to be passed, many young hopefuls sometimes never get past this stage.

The next big problem is when they have a shiny new commercial flying licence, with little or no experience, who will employ them? That can be difficult. Many of the larger airlines that have their own sponsored programmes employ them as second officers, doing much of the more mundane chores but observing and building experience, which is an essential part of their learning curve. Time passes, experience is gained and eventually after good assessments they progress to become a first officer, who will take his place in the right hand seat of the cockpit, next to the captain on the left.

All pilots have continual medical examinations, twice a year over forty years old and have regular training and assessments in the simulator to practise all the worst possible scenarios that could occur so that should an unlikely event ever happen they will be prepared to cope calmly and professionally. It takes many years to progress to becoming a captain of an airliner and often the progression is from smaller to larger types. The unseen crew in the front of your aircraft have not only yours but of course their own well being at heart, but they don't see it that way because to them it is a job of work, to be carried out professionally, they have the confidence in themselves knowing they have a full understanding of their aeroplane and how to deal with any unforeseen circumstance.

Ask yourself this question who would you prefer to be sitting in the cockpit; yourself or well-trained pilots, if you were there, what input could you have?

One of the more recent advances that came about in Aviation is called "Crew Resource Management" which now means that the old stereotype of cockpit hierarchy with a tyrannical captain and compliant crewmembers has now been erased, instead today the most junior second officer can question the decisions of a captain without fear of rebuke, and the captain now will consider the suggestions of the S/O which might be a far better idea than that of the captain, all flight deck members are now treating each other as competent professionals. Interestingly this same method of management has been adopted in the medical profession for use in the operating theatre, much fewer prima donna's!

So if you feel that you are out of control at least give some thought to the level of competence in front of you. People ask me if I mind travelling as a passenger, I find the answer obvious "of course I don't" because I know that there are professionals in front and I am happy to put my trust in them and relax and enjoy the benefits of the flight.

The Cabin staff

A common misconception about cabin staff is that their prime function is to serve meals and sell duty free goods, well ok, they do these tasks to make the journey more pleasant for the passenger, but that is not the prime role. Like pilots the cabin staff have to have extensive training in emergency procedures, and their objective is the safety of the passengers in any situation. First aid and fire fighting training is essential and also how to deal with passengers and their worries. Not only do the attendants have regular training and checks in safety and emergency procedures, but also they will have a pre flight oral examination from the senior cabin staff member to ensure their standard is up to scratch prior to flight. Quite often a reassurance from an understanding cabin attendant can make all the difference to a fearful passenger.

The Aircraft engineer

Here is someone who I respect and has my admiration as an unsung hero, he will work on the aeroplane in all atrocious weathers, rain, sleet snow, sub zero temperatures or blazing sun with sapping humidity, trying to rectify minor snags or carrying out routine maintenance, often in the small hours of the night. He is a highly trained dedicated technician working on modern aircraft at the forefront of technology, his skills when working are a joy to watch and fill me with confidence in knowing he has done a better job than I could ever have hoped to do.

Air traffic controllers

We have an idea from films and television of an air traffic controller as a person at the top of a control tower holding a microphone standing up, looking out into the distance talking aeroplanes down. That might have been how it looked in the 20's and 30's or 40's but nothing could be further from the truth today.

Air traffic today is a highly integrated system of control; which links across continents and countries seamlessly, in fact the air above the whole globe is inter-connected.

An aircraft flying from point 'a' anywhere in the world to point 'b' anywhere else will be under control at all times. The people, who integrate this system and keep aircraft separated, have been through a system of training not dissimilar to pilots.

They also need to be physically fit; they need to have a thorough understanding of the needs for control and how to apply them. Modern equipment is at their disposal and they have to know how to use it and how it works, they also have proficiency assessments and are monitored and trained to maintain a high standard of professionalism. Read more about them in the chapter on Air Traffic Control.

Airports

There are a multitude of people at the airport who are visible to the traveller and those who work behind the scenes. Examples of the former are the security police who have a high profile and are prolific, the check in staff who will ask you questions about your baggage and simple personal security, immigration and security staff, agents at the departure gate. Of the latter there are the baggage handlers who load your bags onto your aircraft, the marshallers, aircraft refuellers, airline ramp agents, maintenance personnel, bus drivers, etc. All these people apart from carrying out their appointed tasks are trained to be security conscious, so there exists another layer of unseen security between arrival at the airport and departure of the aircraft.

The Controlling Authorities

All countries of the world will have a governing body whose responsibility it is to oversee the regulation of aviation in all its forms. Some people might say it is just another bureaucratic organisation being a burden on the taxpayer of that country, but wait, there is a positive side to this.

Aviation exists in every country and there needs to be a body who will police the activities of the industry. Which exists in areas of manufacture, maintenance, operation, training, licensing, etc, by imposing safety regulations and making the adherence and application of them law, for the ultimate safety of the travelling public. As we saw before, aviation is a wide all-encompassing industry; which has a multitude of facets.

Some as we have seen do carry an element of risk, examples are crop spraying, air shows, aerobatics, air races, parachuting, here the authorities have a duty to make rules which protect the wider public on the ground. Where newer technology that has a positive bearing on safety becomes available, the controlling bodies have the authority to force the introduction and use, regardless of cost upon aircraft operators within their jurisdiction. There is an overall body called ICAO (the international civil aviation organisation); which was formed after world war two in Chicago where a charter for air transport was drawn up called not unsurprisingly, the Chicago Convention and just about every country now is a member. Next time you buy an airline ticket look on the back, it tells you some of the things about it, for example how much you will be compensated if your baggage gets lost! It does happen, so keep your valuables with you.

The names of a few of the global authorities for example are,

Europe	EASA	European Air Safety Authority
USA	FAA	Federal Aviation Authority
UK	CAA	Civil Aviation Authority

Australia	CASA	Civil Aviation Safety Authority
France	DGAC	Directeur General d'Aviation Civile
Netherlands	RLD	Rijks Luchtvaart Dienst

So the obvious conclusion we can draw from a brief look at those involved in airline operations is that one thing is paramount above all others and that is safety. It has become the cornerstone of aviation and thank goodness there is no complacency in this area of the industry.

Air Traffic Control

All over the world in the skies above us reaching vertically upwards to ten miles or16 kilometres high is a network of air routes that cross each other at intersections. These routes have many different levels, like lots of lanes on a major road, however they are stacked upwards. It's possible to fly from one major airport in the world to another in the world flying on these highways in the sky. The purpose of these airways as they are called is to enable aircraft to safely transit the airspace of a country under control, that control means giving an aircraft a block of airspace around it which will keep it clear both vertically and horizontally from other aircraft, who in turn have their own piece of protected airspace.

In many of the countries the airways are closely monitored on radar by a controller on the ground that will see all the aircraft in his sector of responsibility, he can see them represented as a blip moving across a large TV screen: between the outlines of the airways. The blips have a group of numbers alongside which move with the blip or "return" and they give the controller information about the aeroplane such as, flight number, altitude, speed, and the departure and destination point.

The controller will know to an exact time, the arrival of an aeroplane into his sector, because he will have been advised by the previous sector's controller by either, land line (phone), telex, radio communication or he may even be sitting next to him. Sometimes whole countries are controlled from within one large room, or they can be split into areas where remote radar sensors relay the information back to a central nerve centre,

The controllers know about a particular flight because of a "flight plan" which is just what it says, a filed report with air traffic control at the point of departure of a predicted flight, giving time of departure, the route required, the speed and altitude to be flown, times when leaving and entering a different country's airspace, the time of arrival at destination, number of passengers and crew, type of aircraft, total flight endurance, navigation equipment carried, the captains name, what he had for breakfast (no not really)and just in case the weather should be completely unsuitable or the airport should close; a set of alternate airports. This flight plan is sent telegraphically to all the air traffic control units along the intended track of the airliner so that everyone knows they are coming, where and when, together with their own piece of protected airspace. There is a requirement for the aircraft's operating crews to maintain accurately their time over a particular reporting point and if unable do that because of lets say stronger than predicted winds, they will inform air traffic control of their new estimates which will be passed on.

The function of the individual air traffic controller is to maintain the separation required by all the aircraft in his sector. He can achieve this by instructing the pilots to adjust their speed, change their altitude, or to fly a slightly different route. There are times when many aircraft want to cruise at the same altitude so he will have to consider the needs of each aircraft and adjust on a priority basis.

Over large oceans like the Pacific or Atlantic, or Indian Ocean there are no radar sites so a different approach is employed which is called "procedural", a controller exists but he cannot see the aeroplane, he communicates with them by long range radio or satellite, and based upon the estimates at certain reporting points along the way, together with a larger piece of protected airspace, he can effectively carry out his task of aircraft separation.

In today's modern airliners the navigational equipment is so sophisticated that it is accurate to a few feet and to a few seconds, there is inbuilt redundancy so that should a system fail in mid-ocean there is always an accurate backup, and should the highly unlikely occur whereby all systems are lost, then of course there is the pilot (lets not forget him) one of them continually runs a manual plan along the route on a plotting chart (a sophisticated map) so that flight could continue using what is called dead reckoning. When over land there are additional navigational aids, placed on the ground at turning points or junctions on airways, so that progress can be continuously monitored.

When in flight you will generally see other aircraft out of the windows above or below travelling along the same airway, and you may see another airliner that appears to be flying alongside, he may well be one or two thousand feet above or below you but at altitude a Boeing 747 or Airbus A380 can seem very close indeed when in fact it is a long way off.

When the airliner has started its descent towards the destination airfield it is "handed over" to a controller who is responsible for sequencing inbound aircraft so that they fit into an approach pattern to optimise the number of aircraft able to land on one runway, places like Chicago or Jeddah may have three different runways in use at a time to handle the volume. Both the air traffic controller and pilots form a synergy of true professionals to enable aircraft to land in a continuous sequence of up to one every 20 seconds, in twenty minutes that represents 60 aircraft to be controlled.

I am often asked about "blind landings" no it isn't instruments with Braille on them! But being able to land in minimum forward visibility down to 75 metres (they could land in zero visibility but the pilots have to be able to find their way to the gate after landing!). Modern aircraft have to have this sort of capability in Europe, Canada and North America because of the bad winter fogs, mist and snow showers. With up to three autopilots all cross referring one another and all being monitored by both pilots ready to take over manually, instantaneously should there be a degradation of any of the systems. The pilots have to have been specifically trained and completed many actual approaches first to build up their confidence in the system. Many times practise auto lands are carried out in fine weather to continuously prove the system. And lastly the airport has to have the facilities on the ground; obviously somewhere that rarely sees fog, mist or thick snow is not going to be one of them. If freak weather has arrived at your destination and your pilots cannot carry out an auto land then you will proceed to your alternate if the weather isn't going to clear soon.

You may have heard of "missed approaches or balked landings" these are where the aircraft is not in a position to make a satisfactory landing, for example if a truck entered the far end of the runway (highly unlikely) or the preceding landing aircraft had not cleared the runway, then a go around would be carried out, a bit like taking off again but from a point still in the air, you know your pilots are capable of taking off, they demonstrated that at the beginning of the flight, so its not a problem to them but it may feel uncomfortable to you as you were not expecting it, the worst that can happen is you might miss your train or bus connection.

Another situation I have seen that is perfectly normal but it can cause concern in anxious passengers. Shortly after take-off the departure procedures for busy airports like for example London's Heathrow, New York's Kennedy, Chicago's O Hare, Amsterdam's Schipol airport may require a departing aircraft to maintain a specific altitude until passing a prescribed distance from the airport due to the arrival procedures of aircraft overhead. So after climbing at maximum angle at full power in order to keep the noise level close to the airport the departing aircraft is now required to fly level so a large pitch change downwards together with a large reduction in power can leave the worried passenger in a state of anxiety, so if it happens to you, you will know exactly what is happening and feel calm and collected.

Weather and Turbulence

Weather is something we live with on a day-to-day basis and accept that it has its vagaries and depending on the time of year and place, it can give us four seasons of weather in one day! Vancouver Canada is a good example. Similarly our aeroplane can experience all the extremes of weather that could be thrown at it whilst we inside sit in comfort oblivious to the environment outside the window.

The environment an aeroplane travels in is well known to the designer and of course all aircraft are rigorously designed with this in mind. We sit inside our cars at a comfortable 24c degrees whilst outside it could be –10c or +35c, we think nothing these days about climate control and accept is as normal. The climate control in an aeroplane works in a similar manner except at cruising altitude the temperature can go as low as -65c and then to land in a desert environment where the temperature can be at +40C, the difference being the boiling point of water! Around the world at the tropopause, which occurs around 37,000 feet the temperature remains stable at about –65c regardless of whether there is a desert or pole below. Pretty hostile environment, especially when we consider that there is very little oxygen in the air at these levels, also the air pressure is very low, which is why we have to make an environment that is comfortable to us. By pressurising the air from outside we increase also the oxygen content to an equivalent level of about 8000 feet inside, like say the skiing slopes of the Alps. Because the air has been pressurised it warms up and we can then make the cabin temperature a comfortable level. Should you feel hot or cold on a flight, ask the cabin attendant to adjust it, they will generally accommodate your wishes.

The air is in constant motion around the globe, because the world is turning and because the air is rising and falling as it heats and cools, from region to region and between pressure systems that form and decline locally within a region. The air moves in a similar way to water in a stream with eddies and whirls as it moves over rocks and boulders, the effects of mountains and obstructions will be felt through a deeper layer because of it being less dense. So those whirls and eddies of the air are felt by the people inside their aeroplane as turbulence, but remember turbulence is only felt occasionally and then hardly enough to spill our drinks. The worried passenger may well start to grip the seat and begin to fear the integrity of the aeroplane and at worst fear for their safety. All they need to do is look across the aisle at the regular traveller who hasn't even noticed the disturbance and may well carry on reading his newspaper; often the captain does not deem it necessary to ask the passengers to fasten their seatbelts.

But for the anxious passenger, turbulence in any form can heighten those anxieties, unless he understands the mechanisms involved.

Those mechanisms start at the factory; the designers know all about turbulence, they know it exists and it is always likely that it could be encountered and so **they design the aircraft to be strong enough to withstand <u>far more</u> than any turbulence that could ever be experienced in routine airline operations.**

It may well be very uncomfortable and you may well have to put your seatbelt on, but it won't harm you.

The sort of turbulence that exists in films associated with thunder storms is avoided by the use of modern aircraft weather radar technology and efficient weather forecasting; remember pilots don't like to be uncomfortable either and so they always fly around that sort of weather and turbulence, and what's more the cruising levels are higher than the weather. A point worth bearing in mind is that aircraft are designed again to be able to cope with lightning strikes, the principle of the "Faraday" box applies here, just like in your car, if you are inside a metal compartment that is struck by lightning you are safe as so is everything else inside. It does make a loud crack, I know I've heard it many, many times before in flight but that's about all it does, but as I said that sort of weather is always avoided. The winds associated with jet streams can give rise to turbulence but it is usually of a short duration and plenty of warning is given by the pilots to finish your drink. The other type of turbulence is low level; which is felt on approach to landing where wind near the ground is being made choppy by hills, buildings, cliffs, woods etc, again this is something of a normal occurrence to pilots and dealing with it is regarded as part of their basic flying abilities and nothing to have any concerns about.

I have been asked about "air pockets", well actually there is no such thing, it's just a couple of words that mean bumps of turbulence, people even say they dropped 10,000 feet! How would they know? Actually the aircraft will only have changed by a few feet as it flies through rising and descending air masses that try to push it up or down. The slower we fly the more we can reduce the effects of turbulence, which is why your pilots will sometimes reduce power to slow down and make it less uncomfortable.

So let's keep in mind that the aeroplane structure is designed to cope with more turbulence than you are ever likely to encounter, uncomfortable as it may be. By practising the techniques you will learn later in "coping strategies" you will be able to deal with it successfully.

The Landing

So there you are, comfortably sitting in your seat feeling the aeroplane gradually descending lower and lower, and as you look out of the window the ground is gradually getting closer and closer, and you might wonder where the runway is? Well of course you can't see it because it is in front of the aeroplane and the view you have from the cabin window is sideways. But eventually you can see houses and fields gradually becoming larger and larger, and eventually you see the concrete and the start of the runway slowly but surely getting closer to you.

Then with a rumble and maybe even a very slight bump, the aircraft is on the runway and the next thing you hear is a loud noise from the engines, which is the reverse thrust. Reverse thrust is used on just about every landing as the power from the engines is directed forwards which also helps to slow the aircraft down and use less wheel brakes, which in turn makes the brakes last longer and less costly in brake replacement (don't forget airlines have to make a profit or they wouldn't be there to take us anywhere)

When travelling as a passenger just after touchdown I have heard a burst of applause from around the cabin, could this be relief? Or could it be appreciation of a superbly smooth landing? Either way the pilots up front in the cockpit sadly can't hear what is going on in the cabin, but I'm sure they would like to think it's the latter.

As we saw earlier air traffic control works together with the flight crew to help position the aircraft in sequence to begin their approach to landing, but how is this achieved?

At most larger airports each runway has an **instrument landing system** referred to as an **ILS**, which sends out electronic beams both vertically and horizontally, the horizontal one is angled normally at 3 degrees upwards from the point of touchdown, and vertically in line with the centre of the runway, so that it forms a gradually narrowing cone to the touchdown point on the centre of the runway at the correct distance from the beginning of the concrete. At most airports with an ILS there would be a locator beacon, which sends out a signal enabling aircraft to home to it, this is generally aligned with the runway some distance out from the touch down point, or even at the airport itself. The purpose of this beacon is to enable the pilots to start their published arrival procedures. The arrival procedure commences at a prescribed height at the locator beacon, there's a turn to a prescribed direction followed by a descent to another prescribed height. The pilots then make a turn at a certain time or distance from the beacon back towards the runway, the turn is like a long teardrop shape which will have the aircraft "established" on the centreline of the ILS, they will then fly towards the runway until they intercept that 3 degree descent (glideslope) and start a gradual descent usually lowering the landing gear and final stages of flaps at this point.

Just before the aircraft touches down (about 1 to 2 feet above the ground) the pilots will close the engine throttles and now it all goes quiet, which is a big difference from the flaps and landing gear going down and all the power changes a few minutes ago. Now the aeroplane is allowed to sink gently to the ground and just as it does touch the ground the noise starts again as the reverse thrust is actuated, we can all feel the brakes being applied just as we could in a car, slowing us until we come to slow taxying speed and turn off the runway.

Nothing to it is there!! Well ok I know it isn't all as simple as that, however there are many different types of approach using different types of approach aids and now of course very accurate Global Positioning Systems (GPS) which together with ILS can give accuracies to within a few centimetres.

I have been asked many times "how on earth do you manage to land in fog?" yes that is a valid question. Remember all pilots have to be able to fly on instruments and be able to carry out approaches in cloud down to a low height without any visual references to the ground, just using the instruments in front of them. Generally speaking the visibility should be equal to or better than 550 metres or a quarter of a mile and the cloud base in the order of 200 feet above the runway, so that the last stages of the flight can be conducted with visual reference to the runway. But it isn't always like that and the cloud can be down to the ground with visibility much lower than 100 metres, you most probably wouldn't go out in your car in those conditions!

So how do they land in those poor visibility conditions? Well, in the early 60's there was an aeroplane called the Trident operated by BEA (British European Airways) before it was amalgamated with BOAC (British Overseas Airways Corporation) later to become British Airways (BA). This aeroplane was the very first that had the capability of making auto landings at London's Heathrow airport.

Since those early days the equipment has become ultimately more sophisticated, and worldwide now modern airliners have the capability to auto land.

There are many requirements to comply with before an auto land can be attempted. Firstly the aeroplane has to have the ability to cope with several compounded failures within each of its crucial systems, so that a failure of any component or system at a critical part of the approach would not compromise that approach. Those systems for example are duplicated and triplicated, such as electrical, hydraulic, navigation, autopilot systems, failure warning systems, etc. etc.

The ILS equipment on the ground has to be of such an accuracy to allow an aircraft to carry out an automatic landing, and its self-monitoring systems also are of the same high standard.

The flight deck crew all have to have had specific training in the simulator with every conceivable failure at the most critical point of the approach, and be able to recognise and deal with any eventuality. They then will have to carry out a required number of auto land approaches in good visual conditions to build confidence in their learned capabilities and also the technology.

During an automatic approach, the aircraft systems are flying the aircraft down the ILS, however the Captain has his hands on the aircraft and engine controls ready to take over control of the aeroplane at any second, and both pilots are constantly monitoring the systems and instruments and also each other. The aircrafts autopilots will level the aircraft just above the runway, make a gentle touchdown and bring the aeroplane to a halt on the runway. There needs to be a minimum visibility in the order of 70 metres to be able to taxy the aircraft off the runway, along the taxiways to the parking gate. It could be very embarrassing for the pilots to get lost; at larger airports there is ground movement radar, which enables air traffic control to assist aircraft in taxying around the airport in bad visibility and also to see where everyone is situated to help avoid a traffic jam and the embarrassment of two jumbo jets coming face to face on a taxiway.

Because of the sensitivity of all the electronic airborne and ground equipment involved, a greater separation is needed between aircraft making their approaches to land so that no electronic interference can occur. This separation inevitably means less aircraft can land in a given period of time, which in turn means delays to arrivals with aircraft having to enter a holding pattern until their turn to start the approach to land. This might sound complicated but it's something that all airline pilots are familiar with and carry out these procedures nearly everyday of their working lives.

Having said all that there are parts of the world where fog hardly ever occurs, and as a result there is no need for sophisticated landing systems like automatic landing capabilities, however the pilots still have to be able to carry out those procedures because aviation is a global industry and they could be faced with bad weather conditions in many parts of the world.

Terrorism and Security

Since that wake up call of 9/11, aviation security has been through a momentous shake-up. Prior to that date we never thought that an aeroplane could be used in the way that the terrorists used it: as a weapon. Since then the world of security took a new and radical view towards passengers. Since that date they are now scrutinised in a way like never before and that of course is towards the benefit of everyone.

There were many knee jerk reactions to security in the aftermath of 9/11 but now several years later and many lessons learned we have in place an integrated international system of protection. Although there had been many terrorist incidents in the past before 9/11 with aircraft hijackings, nothing had quite brought home to the world and importantly to the United States how vulnerable it was to attacks from within its own territory, by congressional decree something had to be done.

The initial response was to set up a system of enhanced aircraft security whereby access to the flight deck area was denied to anyone. Now on all airliners globally there are bulletproof doors with sophisticated locking and secure operating systems, which deny access to all but the operating crew. Don't worry about what should happen if your pilot becomes ill because there are always two pilots in the cockpit, both perfectly qualified to operate your aeroplane, and what's more they are required to eat different meals just in case of the highly unlikely event of food poisoning. The aircraft is always checked over by security staff and then again by the operating crew before the day commences to ensure there is nothing suspicious on board and again before each successive flight.

Another measure that was introduced in some countries was armed sky marshals that travel on the flight incognito as normal passengers. Towards the end of 2005 a passenger in Miami airport who was behaving suspiciously and shouting that he was carrying a bomb, tried to make his way to an aeroplane, whereupon he was shot dead by a sky marshal. It transpired there was no bomb and the person was mentally deranged. Obviously there wasn't a bomb because it would have shown up on the airport security systems, but very reassuring to know that another layer of unseen protection exists.

The airports have adopted a system of measures that are both passive and active that increase levels of security to the highest order. Many airports will screen all baggage; both hand and hold baggage prior to entry into the airport itself. Check in staff will ask relevant questions of the passenger about heir baggage and what they are carrying, the passengers will have maybe up to two more electronic hand baggage and personal checks to go through. Airports now have cameras that photograph all the passengers who are then computer scanned against known individuals; armed police and security staff patrol all areas of the airport. The hold baggage is all now x-rayed and even sniffer dogs give it a once over. The personal profile of all airport employees is highly scrutinised and checked before any are considered for employment and all are trained in security.

So I think you would agree that everything possible to make the flight secure from unwanted individuals is being done and that air travel is now the most secure way to travel. Sadly that point has been made by the Bali bombings, the train bombings in Madrid and the tube and bus bombings in London, the Ba Ta Clan bombing in Paris, the Boston marathon bombing. It is a sad indictment of the world in which we live that nowhere in any aspect of our lives are we safe from the terrorists in our own corner of the globe as we go about our daily affairs. The one really reassuring point is that now we can relax in the knowledge that as we have come to accept an element of risk from terrorists in our everyday lives, air travel gives us a temporary sanctuary from the madness that exists on the ground.

Aviation Health

Although good health is important to us all there are some aspects of health related issues in flying, that by having a simple understanding can make our journeys that much more comfortable.

Before you leave home

The first thing any worried passenger needs to avoid is stressing them selves unnecessarily, start your journey well ahead of time so that you arrive at the airport in plenty of time, give yourself a chance to book a seat that you would prefer. With the extra security measures now in place, you should allow extra time anyway. If you are taking any medications remember to take plenty for your stay and the return journey and also take a list of what they are in case you need any more while away. Don't put yourself in the embarrassing position of remembering you left your heart pills at home just before the doors close for departure.

Clothing

Wear something comfortable, I know that sounds an obvious thing to say, but at altitude, inside the reduced pressure of the aeroplane the body can bloat a little, so wear loose fitting shoes, loosely elasticated clothing and think about how the weather will be when you step outside at your destination, so carry something suitable. I have taken people from the Caribbean; where they have boarded in shorts and a tee shirt, only to arrive at the destination where it was sub-zero and snowing, you should have seen the look on their faces!

A good idea on long flights, although it is very tempting is to avoid alcohol and fizzy drinks, because the pressure is reduced at altitude the effect of the bubbles in gassy drinks will be much greater so you could get wind and stomach cramps which could be painful, alcohol's effect also increases greatly with altitude and even more importantly the dehydrating effect of both that and the reduced moisture in the air means that if we don't drink more water we could feel a bit under the weather. The skin will give up moisture really quickly and start to dry out, which is why a moisturiser and drinking more water is again a good idea.

Exercise

One of the most recently publicised problems with air travel called economy class syndrome, or DVT (deep vein thrombosis) isn't really a function of air travel solely but inactivity encountered with any form of travel for long periods, bus, train or whatever. Blood pools in the lower legs where in susceptible people it could cause a small clot, which can then travel around the blood system, getting stuck in say the lungs to cause a pulmonary embolism or in the brain to cause a stroke. What can you do? Several things, get up and walk around as often as you can, try and put your carry on bag under the seat in front below your feet to raise them up, do muscle tensing exercises in the calves, tense really hard all the muscles in the calves, ankles and thighs and hold for a few seconds and then relax, repeat again for a few times and do this at regular intervals, you could buy a pair of flight socks which squeeze the calves reducing the possibility of blood pooling.

The Ears

Some people really have difficulty with their ears on a flight, most often during the descent. Should you travel with a cold it can affect them painfully. The purpose of the eardrums is to be able hear and keep water from inside our heads! I know with some people that's all there is inside!! Because sound travels through the air and vibrates the eardrum, it needs to be kept at the same pressure inside it as outside or our hearing would be impaired, so this tiny tube called the Eustachian tube connects the inner ear to the inside of our throats and most of the time as the air pressure changes throughout the day gradually so the pressure balance is maintained. During flight we experience greater and faster pressure changes than normal so the pressure equalisation system has to work more.

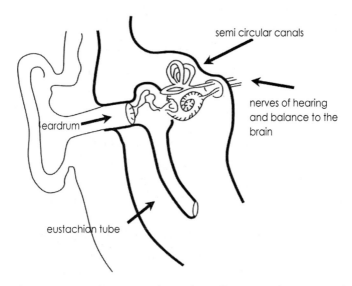

semi circular canals

nerves of hearing
and balance to the
brain

eardrum

eustachian tube

Diagram 6. The ear showing the eardrum and Eustachian tube

If we develop a cold those tiny tubes can become inflamed and close up, thus it becomes difficult to equalise the pressure in the ear and the eardrum gets stretched which can be very painful. A known way to force clear the ears (but not if you have a cold) is to do the Valsalva method, which is; squeeze the nose with thumb and forefinger, close the mouth, relax the throat and try and blow into your nose and throat, hopefully your ears should clear with a pop, no guarantees though, and if it doesn't work then you will have to ask everyone to talk up a little! It will usually clear in day or so, but basically try not to fly with a cold. Often small babies will start to cry on descent, what the parent can do is give them a bottle of what they drink as the swallowing effect helps to equalise the pressure. A long time ago the cabin attendants would offer a boiled sweet to the passengers just before commencing descent to help clearing the ears by swallowing.

Interestingly the ear has another function, it contains the balance mechanism which if incorrectly disturbed can make us feel sick. Deep inside the ear are three semi circular canals set in three axes of movement, which contain a fluid that moves in the same way that we move, that motion is felt by tiny hairs called cilia which in turn send messages to the brain telling us about our motion. Our eyes see a picture, which interprets a correct sign for motion, and this is all correlated in the brain to confirm what we feel and what we see as correct. For example as we drive off in a car, we know we should feel acceleration, the appropriate semi circular canal sends sensory information to the brain and it confirms the picture from the eyes. Now then if we send a picture to the brain that doesn't confirm what our ears are telling us, the brain can't resolve this and the end result is we start to feel nauseous and disorientated. It's very easy to confuse our inner ears, remember the roundabout as children, spinning round and round then getting off and trying to stand up straight and of course falling down, the fluid in the ear hadn't settled. The same thing can happen on boats and planes and cars if we can't see a visual reference and have continually differing motion, then it's just like the roundabout, disorientation and sickness. You can sit by the window and look out each time the plane banks to look below at the ground, which will help to keep a visual reference. But generally manoeuvres are carried out so gently as to be almost unnoticeable.

Jet lag is a problem that few regular travellers can get to grips with; there are some helpful techniques to lessen the problem.

What is jet lag? Our bodies are designed to function in a normal 24-hour (in fact it is really a 25 hour period called a circadian cycle) system with night and day following a regular pattern adjusted for seasonal differences. Our bodies regulate our functions according to the time of day, generally we wake in the morning and feel tired in the evening and sleep through the night. If we transport ourselves to a time zone that is say twelve hours difference then we would find it difficult to stay awake during the day and sleep at night. Effectively this is what air travel does to us; takes us out of our normal rhythm and puts into a different time zone where we cannot immediately adjust. It is normally accepted that we can accept two hours difference without too much trouble and the body will adjust to the new time zone at a rate of approximately one hour per day. So for example if we travel to the west coast of America from the United Kingdom or vice versa the difference is 8 hours, so then less the two hours we can adjust, it then leaves six days to be totally adjusted. What some business people that are only going for a few days will do, is stay in their own time zone, i.e. go to bed and get up at the time they would have done before they left; which means when they get back home there is no jet lag. The disadvantage is that when you are up and about the rest of the population is in bed asleep, and when you are asleep that's a good time for noisy hotel maintenance! There was a time when the drug Melatonin was recommended for jetlag, however now in some countries like the UK it is not available and not enough clinical trials on the drug, jetlag and side effects have been carried out, although it is available in the USA.

When travelling on vacation, don't leave your senses behind at home, don't drink to excess, think safely, take normal precautions and don't do anything you wouldn't do at home, except have a wonderful time.

Relaxation

Why do most programmes about fear of flying have in them an element concerned with relaxation? Based upon the principle of *reciprocal inhibition* which states that anxiety cannot co-exist with other emotional conditions such as: hunger, thirst, sexual arousal and relaxation. So wouldn't it seem rational to induce a state that would inhibit anxiety? Obviously we don't want to make ourselves feel hungry and thirsty and we wouldn't want to be in a state of sexual arousal before going flying, would we? So a relaxed state is the best state to be in to help overcome our anxiety. As we know fear creates a state of tension in the muscles (preparedness for the fight or run-away response), which in turn leads to stress, as we know de-stressing and relaxation are synonymous, so the answer is to be in a state of relaxation or know how to get to into it if we find ourselves to be in an anxiety provoking situation.

We all have the means by which we can relax, for some it is reading a book, listening to music, watching a movie, having a drink or doing a crossword puzzle, or you could learn a few techniques to help achieve a state of relaxation wherever you are, where you don't need anything other than yourself to achieve it.

In normal everyday life our muscles are used continuously quite often without knowing that we are using them and within those muscles are nerves; which in turn send signals to the brain, there is an interpretation by the brain of the muscle tension and what it is doing for the individual. A coffee cup in front of you is being lifted to your lips, a whole raft of muscles come into play, in the arm, the face, the throat, the oesophagus, the digestion system, etc, all naturally working in harmony, the voluntary and autonomic systems. The voluntary muscles are the ones we control by our thoughts, i.e. lifting the glass to our lips, the autonomic, control those parts of our bodies that function without conscious or subconscious thought. Thought processes work back the other way to the muscles, if we are in a perceived stressful situation the muscles will become tense; imagine a drive in heavy traffic at rush hour, enough to make anyone feel tense and anxious. What do you do when you arrive at your destination? Relax in some way, maybe a coffee or a drink or a soak in a hot bath.

If flying is regarded as threatening then any thoughts about flying can give rise to muscle tension in exactly the same way. By use of a deep form of progressive relaxation, muscle tension can be reduced and as we have seen earlier, so will the anxiety. Research has shown, and it is now widely accepted, that relaxation has an effect upon the autonomic nervous system whereby the heart rate will slow and blood pressure decreases, again it has been shown in experiments by the use of heart rate monitors that consciously thinking the heart rate down can achieve that result.

So how do we achieve this form of progressive relaxation? Initially we need to practise the technique so that we can use it either as prevention or for use when we find ourselves in an anxiety-provoking situation.

The Technique

The principal is to physically tense a muscle group, hold it for a few seconds and then relax, at the same time saying to oneself "relax" gradually working around the muscle groups of the body. The purpose of this is to become aware of the contrast between tension and relaxation. Eventually we will feel where the tension exists and be able to eliminate it by concentrating on a specific group of muscles. One should exercise care when tensing the muscles and not overdo it if they should suffer from arthritis or other joint related problems.

Step 1

To start the practise, find a quiet place where you will not be disturbed, remove as many distractions as possible, like a ticking clock, take the phone off the hook, make yourself as comfortable as possible, either laying down or sitting in an armchair. Close your eyes to remove any visual distractions, and now start to take deep breaths and pausing for four or five seconds between inhaling slowly through the nose and exhaling slowly through the mouth, trying to take the breath deep down towards the stomach.

Step 2
The idea now is to try and let your mind go blank, this can be difficult if you have intrusive thoughts that keep popping up, you could try to imagine you are in front of a TV screen and everything you visualise including those thoughts are on that TV, now imagine you switch off the TV and you are looking at a blank screen, concentrate on that screen staying blank.

Step 3
Now start to work sequentially on the muscle groups, the hands and fingers making a fist, tighten the forearms and shoulders, all being kept in tension while you hold your breath for about the count of four, then exhale as you relax the tension, saying in your mind "relax". You can really feel the muscles relax. Now work your way around the body doing the same procedure with the different groups of muscles. Now do the back by arching it, the neck and shoulders by raising the shoulders and pushing the head back, the jaw and tongue, -push the tongue against the roof of the mouth and clench the teeth but be careful not to overdo it, in case you damage crowns or dentures. Screw up your face as

though a bucket of water is being thrown at it. Now work downwards, stomach, buttocks and thighs, calves feet and ankles, curl the toes and point the feet down.

If you can practise this each day it should become easier, and gradually you will be able to apply this technique to any part of your body that is feeling tense. I used to practise this on a long flight in the cruise whilst sitting in the pilots seat as a way of exercise and relaxation together; obviously the other pilot was at the controls at the time.
By now you will be able to relax without tensing the muscle groups first, because you will have become familiar with the sensations of relaxation and know when you have achieved it.

You can use relaxation as a tool, just like the one, which is used by hypnotherapists and psychologists in the treatment of phobias, it is called systematic desensitisation and it works as its name suggests, in which the patient gradually becomes desensitised to the fear making stimulus, in our case flying.

By now you should know when tension begins to build and you should know when you are relaxed. If when you are completely relaxed start to think of an image that is connected with flying that is not too anxious making, for example packing a case for a flight, and concentrate on relaxing, as you focus on that thought. Now think of something a little more anxiety making and try to relax again as you keep that thought in your mind, for example arriving at the airport. Try Again, as you are able to relax, bring up another image, say walking towards the aeroplane and concentrate on relaxing. You can see that you will gradually be able to feel relaxed with increasing amounts of anxiety about the flight. It can help if you can make a list that is called a hierarchy of anxiety going from 0 to 100, where 0 is no anxiety at all and 100 is the most terrifying thing you can imagine about flying, and gradually fill in the spaces in a graded escalation. Now the thing to do is to set yourself a goal that you would feel happy to achieve, make it realistic and not too ambitious, lets say for example, sitting in a plane with the engines running. Work towards that goal of being able to visualise yourself sitting there feeling relaxed. When you eventually get to feel comfortable with that goal, it is the time to plan a newer slightly more challenging one, let's say being in the cruise in the plane. What you are learning to do is to control your emotional responses to what you thought were fear making situations.

Remember what we said earlier about fear; fear response is strengthened every time we avoid a fearfully perceived situation. Now we have broken that cycle by visiting what we perceived in our hierarchy of anxiety as a fearful situation and staying there and relaxing as we do. It requires practise and perseverance and a sense of determination to achieve the goal, you are going to have to work at it! Don't be put off, if it all doesn't happen right away, countless people before you have achieved their goals, so can you.

Coping Strategies

I hope that by now you have grasped something positive towards beating your fear of flying, it certainly hasn't been easy for you and although you may well have decided to take the plunge and book that first flight, you could be now nervously anticipating that experience. THAT'S OK, if you haven't flown before it is a perfectly natural way to be, and in this chapter I will try to give you some tips on how to get by. These tips work equally well for someone who has flown before but doesn't enjoy the experience. So what are we going to try and do.

First we will stop *catastrophising*, by that I mean stop thinking that the worst will happen to us, this sort of negative thinking gets us nowhere. If you think for example, the wing will fall off or you will crash or get hijacked, where's the evidence for this, do you have a crystal ball? Are you psychic? You know you can't predict the future. It's not as though this has happened to you before, you have to take control of your thoughts, start to challenge them and dispute anything that you really know doesn't make sense (read the statistics chapter again), it does take a conscious effort of will to stop a negative train of thought and forget the "what if" about the future and think about the present. Why let negative thoughts about what could happen spoil the present?

Isn't it better to think instead about the good things of the present, and that should start to make you feel good.

A way to stop those unwanted thoughts taking root is to replace them immediately by a physical and mental process. You can put a rubber band around your wrist and pull it out and then let go of it, that should stop a train of thought, and at the same time think of yourself shouting "stop" or you could think of a big red stop sign right in front of you, either way you most certainly will have stopped thinking about whatever it was. If the thought persists, try pulling the rubber band out further before letting go, ouch!

An experiment with a group of people demonstrates the principal works. I get them to close their eyes and then start thinking of something really fearful, I then pick up a heavy book and crash it down on the table, naturally they all open their eyes to see what it was, then I ask them what they are now thinking about, yes, you guessed it, no-one is thinking about those fearful thoughts. All we are doing with thought stopping on the aircraft is much the same thing, using a *distraction* technique of our own. Some people fear they might have a panic attack and even fear they may disgrace themselves in front of others, so what is a panic attack all about and what can be done about it?

In a situation like flying a person could start to feel anxious about a simple event, for example a noise that they perceive as a signal of danger, their usual reaction would be escape, however they are unable to do that and feel trapped, the body starts to react to the fight or flight mechanism by producing changes in the body such as, sweating, heart rate increasing, breathing rate increasing and shallow, muscles tense, blood pressure rises, eventually the person can feel as if they are going to have a heart attack or die, actually the very worst thing that can happen is they will faint and the body mechanism goes back to normal, unpleasant as it is, it is not life threatening. So what do you do if you find yourself starting to go into panic mode?

First thing is to control your breathing, close your mouth and take slow deep breaths through your nose, which will help you to stop hyperventilating, immediately start your own distracting technique and start to concentrate on the relaxation method you learned earlier, stay with it and work at it.

An important thing to do is approach the idea of flying from a different viewpoint, lets concentrate on the pleasant aspects of the whole experience, and yes they do exist. From the moment we have decided to take a flight we should be concentrating on why we are taking it, could it be to go on vacation? Visit a relative or friend? Or could it be for work and maybe promotion? Lets think forward to the time we are at our destination and concentrate on the good things we will experience; like the warm sunshine, music, sea and sand, or happy laughter of children and the warm glow of seeing long lost relatives. Keep that picture in mind and keep visiting it, the power of positive thought should not be underestimated.

On the day of departure arrive in plenty of time, security checks now take a lot longer (and that's a good thing), spend some time to visit the shops in the departure lounge, buy something for yourself or buy a present for someone else, have a bite to eat or indulge yourself in one of the many food outlets, buy a book or a magazine, choose some duty free, in fact pamper yourself for a while, it's a great way to distract yourself. Any anxieties that may be creeping in can be dealt with by practising relaxation and thought stopping. If you are travelling with someone else, you could let him or her know how you feel and how you deal with your anxieties and get them to help you to distract your negative thoughts by engaging with you in conversation or doing things.

Once on the plane, you could introduce yourself to a cabin attendant and let them know you are an anxious flyer, they are very sympathetic and will do their best to help you through the flight. Is this flight a long one or a short one? There will be many things to look forward to on either. A short one means you will be able read a newspaper and have a coffee and then you are there at your destination. A longer one means you will be able see some movies, have a meal, read a book, and get some sleep, think when was the last time you had the time to do all those things.

So now you are feeling a little more confident, yes? Good. Let's run through what you could expect on a normal flight. There are going to be mechanical noises which you may not understand and could feel anxious about, so let's talk about those to give you an understanding of them, so that you will be prepared and expect them so they won't come as a surprise.

We talked about landing gear in an earlier chapter and that once airborne they just cause drag and so cost fuel, so they are retracted into the body of the aircraft (about 5-20 seconds after take-off). They are retracted using hydraulic motors; which can make a whirr as they bring up the heavy wheels and legs, when they lock into position they also can make a loud thunk, which you can also feel. The next thing to prepare for is either a short level off, when the engine power is reduced in order to fly level for a short while (just about all airports have departure procedures which may or might not call for this) then continue the climb, or the flaps to be retracted (as the aircraft starts to accelerate), these are operated by screw jacks in the wings, they can be operated by electric or hydraulic motors which are situated under the floor of the cabin and these can also make a whirr, which you can feel. During the climb to altitude it may be necessary to level at an intermediate altitude until the requested one becomes available, this may happen several times, also as fuel is burnt off, the aeroplane becomes lighter and a higher cruising level becomes more economical. So you will hear the engines accelerate as you begin each step climb and retard as you level off. During the flight you may well hear call bells ringing, this is normal and it is just other passengers attracting the attention of the flight attendants for something like a glass of water, a drink, or to buy something or other. There may well be times that the pilots decide to put on the seatbelts sign, and they often will advise you about any turbulence. It may not even be noticeable turbulence but in these litigious times they have to be conscious of any possibilities.

You will usually be told how long you have to go to landing and how long before starting descent; which is when the engines are brought back to idle and the pitch angle changes, you may well experience a very slight buffeting which could be the airbrakes being operated, and towards the latter stages of the flight, the flaps and landing gear just like after take-off. After you smoothly touch down you will hear the loud noise of the thrust reversers operating in the engines and the effect of their deceleration.

If you have managed to control your fear this far you are well on the way to full recovery, remember from the description of phobia the way to beat it is <u>not to avoid</u> it, but to meet it head on, and each time you do, it will diminish until the phobia is either extinguished or you can control it.

Further Help

Although I hope this book will be of use to you in helping you to understand a little about flying and what you can do to help yourself get to grips with a fear of flying, however you may want to seek a little more help before taking the plunge. There are now several treatments available to you that specialise in helping the fearful flyer.

There are courses that are run at many places around the world in many countries by the major airlines themselves that conclude in a short flight, these usually have participants in the order of 100-150 people in order to fill the aeroplane, those courses are usually held at or close to the airport where the flight will take place. There are courses that are designed for smaller numbers of around 10-15 people and these are not necessarily close to the airport.

There are then the treatments for the individual, these are conducted by psychologists and hypnotherapists who offer sessions of treatment that are successful because they are tailored to the person's specific needs. There is now a new type of treatment called Virtual Reality, which enables the patient to experience a passenger flight without leaving the ground. Pilot training simulators are also sometimes used because of their total realism to the aircraft cockpit. Medication is sometimes prescribed by Doctors, to help patients reduce their anxiety, but this is generally not recommended as it just temporarily masks the underlying problem and can have undesirable contra-indications.

All the treatments above will have some common elements, the same as those we have discussed in this book such as.

Cognitive restructuring
Or Cognitive behavioural therapy, which really means changing the way we think about some of our negative emotions and re-evaluating our perceptions.

Information,
By becoming more knowledgeable about the aeroplane, weather, and flying, and so dispelling myths and misconceptions.

Relaxation
An important technique which; helps us deal with negative thoughts and emotions.

Coping strategies
Employing learnt techniques to cope with unwanted reactions to our fear responses.

Flight
This is taken at some stage soon after treatment, in order to self prove and break the circle of avoidance.

Workshops

Seminars or workshops as they are also called, can be run by one person, but it is rare to find someone who will have all the necessary knowledge to pass on. What generally occurs is for a psychologist and an airline pilot to conduct the day's events and cover everything we have discussed in this book. Depending upon the size of the group, individual questions and answers can be covered. Then depending upon the group size, all go to take a short flight of approximately 45 minutes. Generally this works fine but for some people they do need more exposure or a means of systematic desensitisation before the flight. This can be addressed by both hypnosis and psychotherapy as methods of achieving in-vitro (simulated or imagined reality) exposure. Another method utilising near real conditions (near in-vivo) is Virtual Reality exposure. The method the psychologists utilise in in-vitro is asking the patient to visualise progressively more fearful situations and helping the patient to relax with each progression, by using direct suggestions and slow regular breathing exercises. This is effective but can be a lengthy process of treatment. Near In-vivo has the advantage of giving the patient a feeling of total immersion in the environment and they may feel unable to escape, thereby facing head on their anxieties without being able to avoid them. How do they work?

Hypnosis

Actually hypnosis has been used for the treatment of fear of flying and other phobias for a long time. One has to dispense with the idea that hypnotists are all Svengalian characters that have their subjects in their complete power, or indeed stage hypnotists, who seek those extravert individuals to achieve between them solely entertainment value. The true clinical hypnotist has spent years learning how to help individuals with their problems, and in the UK there is a governing body, The British Association for Counselling and Psychotherapy, which sets out guidelines for ethical practise, www.bacp.co.uk/ethicalframework/ for more information.

Or in the USA there is the American Society of Clinical Hypnosis www.asch.net or the American Association of Professional Hypnotherapists www.aaph.org and in Australia the Professional Clinical Hypnotherapists of Australia www.pcha.com.au

During hypnosis the body relaxes and the conscious mind takes a back seat whilst the unconscious mind takes control of the thought processes. The mind can now completely concentrate because all external disturbances and distractions are removed. This is called an *altered state of awareness*; the person knows what is going on, just like that period before we go to sleep, or when intently watching a film or reading an engrossing book, we are not aware of what is happening around us. In the past we may have learned *irrational* fears and as we have seen they can become the shaky foundations upon which our subsequent logic has been built. During hypnosis we have the ability to change the way we respond to what was a previously fearful situation, now we can become completely in control of our emotions. We are able to see ourselves in the future taking a flight and being completely calm and in control of our own emotions and start to feel positive about the whole event. After a session of hypnosis has finished the individual is given homework in the form of relaxation: which they practise at home before their next visit. It's difficult to say exactly how many of these sessions may be required but one to three seem to the norm. In the UK a list of registered clinical hypnotherapists can be obtained from www.bsch.org.uk

Flight Simulators
These are the systems used by pilots in their regular airline training and are at the forefront of technical sophistication and the cost of them can run into several million dollars or pounds. The cost of hiring one of these for a fear of flying exposure treatment is very expensive indeed when taken with the additional cost of people to fly the simulator, costs in 2005/6 can run at around £600 or $1100 an hour, it can also be difficult to obtain a session when one is wanted as they are constantly in use on a regular basis by the airlines. The benefits are that it truthfully replicates visual and

movement cues and sensations from the flight deck and the patient can see the operation of the aircraft from the pilot's viewpoint. The session can be exactly tailored to the individuals need, from turbulence, to take-off and landings

Virtual Flight

The treatment using virtual reality consists of a custom designed virtual environment that has been carefully designed to support exposure therapy in Fear of Flying treatments. This treatment involves exposing the patient to a virtual environment containing the feared situation, (the inside of an aircraft cabin with a window seat) rather than taking the patient into the actual environment or having them imagine being on board. The patient wears sophisticated glasses called visors with TV screens in them which give a realistic image and together with motion sensors, the head movements are matched by the picture seen, through the window there is a real time video of the whole flight from push back at the gate, to take-off, flight and landing and taxi back to the gate. The effects of sounds of talking, crew briefings, engine vibrations and weather and turbulence all combine to make this one of the most effective near in-vivo treatments available. The therapist controls the virtual environment through a keyboard, whereby it is possible to expose the individual gradually and repeatedly to the most feared elements. Obviously this could not be achieved in a real time flight situation. See www.virtuallybetter. com in the United States

The World Wide Web has become a directory for just about everything we could need to know, and help with fear of flying is no exception and by using a search engine, help can be found near to wherever we live. A useful website devoted to phobias in general exists in the UK, it can be found at www. anxietyuk.org.uk or in the USA www.adaa.org Many of the major airlines in the USA, UK, Europe and Australia run a programme called either a seminar or workshop that culminates in a flight, American Airlines, British Airways, Virgin, Quantas, and also many of the low cost carriers etc. However there are programmes designed for smaller groups that are more focussed on the individual needs because not all fearful flyers have the same anxieties, some may be nervous about take off, for others it may be turbulence, banking, climbing, etc, etc, and therefore the treatment although essentially the same can be tailored to the individual. In the UK (To-Fly) used to run workshops for small groups and then a follow up if needed with individual sessions of either hypnotherapy, virtual flight experience in their Virtual Cabin or an escorted flight with one of the low cost carriers.

More Aviation Information
for the technically minded

Ok so now you have an understanding of how an aeroplane flies (chapter 3) that wasn't that difficult was it? Well ok it might have been, but for those of you that would like a little more in-depth understanding of the factors that affect the performance of your flight here goes!

The Atmosphere

Although we can't see it, the air that we breath is real and has physical properties, we can see through it just as we can through water, if we flap our hands we can feel the breeze, it has density as does water, not as much but real enough. Our bodies are designed to live comfortably in air just as fish are designed to live in water. In fact our bodies are subject to a column of air stretching up to space, which exerts a pressure all around us of just under 15psi. The average person has about 2700 square inches of surface area, which equates to about 20 tons, fortunately the same pressure exists inside of us as well or we would explode! As one goes higher in the atmosphere so the pressure drops, at around 18,000 feet or 5.5 Kms, the pressure is about half that at the surface and at around 40,000 feet or about 12 Kms (close to the maximum cruising level of jets) it is around a third. You can see why astronauts need special suits to keep them pressurised in the vacuum of space.

The composition of the atmosphere is made up of around 78% nitrogen and 21% oxygen and around 1% other gases. If we were to climb in an unpressurised aeroplane it would be increasingly harder to breath as the reduced pressure of the air would not be able to allow the oxygen to be pushed across the little alveolar sacs in our lungs to the bloodstream, no matter how deep or rapidly we were to breath. Which is why the aeroplane at altitude needs to be pressurised. Not only does pressure drop with increased altitude but so does the temperature, around 2°C for each 1000 feet until we reach the stratosphere at around 33,000 feet where the temperature remains the same with increasing altitude at around -56°C. Above this level the air is stable and generally above the clouds which form lower down in the Troposphere, which is why jet aircraft fly at this altitude and also because it is more efficient.

The Engine

Most newer generation jet engines are called Fanjet engines, where the big blades at the front of the engine do look like big fan blades and deliver the largest part of the thrust around 60%. Basically a jet engine moves a mass of air at high velocity rearwards. Sir Isaac Newton said "to every action there is an equal and opposite reaction". So the action of air being pushed rearwards at high velocity gives an opposite force (thrust), which is what propels the aircraft. As you can see from the following diagram there are several sections to the engine comprising of sets of compressor blades, which compress the incoming air. Between these blades there are sets of stator blades, which don't move but straighten out the air between each set of compressors. In this diagram there is a low-pressure stage and then a high-pressure stage. Some engines have a third stage as well like the Rolls Royce Trent or RB211. There is a bleed from the compressors that sends compressed air to the pressurisation system, which is then regulated to give a smooth amount of air to the cabin regardless of engine speed. The really highly compressed air now enters a section called the combustion chamber where fuel is squirted in and then set alight with a system of spark plugs, this mixture now expands rapidly and forces its way rearwards and as it continues its journey it spins the turbine blades. These blades are connected by shafts to the compressors. So once the engine is started and fuel continues to be injected into the engine it continues to be self-sustaining.

The principle of combustion is just like what happens in a gasoline- powered car. Suck-squeeze-bang-blow. An air/fuel mixture is introduced into the cylinder, the piston then compresses it; a spark plug ignites the mixture (a mini explosion) then expands forcing the piston back down. This process repeats itself three or four thousand times a minute. Your car could have four, six, eight, twelve cylinders all exploding one after another, all pistons racing up and down connected to a crankshaft which harnesses this process and turns it into a circular motion to drive the wheels. Basically the jet engine has only one moving part; the connecting shaft, okay our example has two of them, one inside the other, and a three stage engine would have three.

They all are revolving on bearings and do not need to reverse direction many thousands of times a minute, like your car engine, so you can imagine they are a far more reliable concept than the internal combustion engine in your car, which is continually trying to tear itself apart!

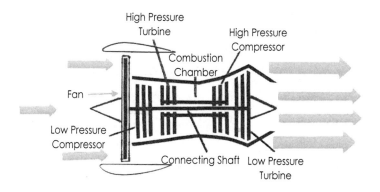

A simplified diagram of a two-stage modern turbofan engine

Preparation before Take Off

Your crew don't just arrive at the aeroplane start the engines and go, if it was that easy we'd all do it. So what do they do? Ok our runway has to be considered individually from all the other runways in the world at the time of departure and all the atmospheric elements at point of departure also have to be considered. The take-off run to the point of lift off varies with factors like temperature, atmospheric pressure, airfield altitude and aircraft weight. The denser the air at a given speed will give more lift to the wings. So a high elevation airfield as we saw earlier where the air is thinner will have less lift at a given speed. Low atmospheric pressure will have the same effect. A high temperature again will have the same effect (air molecules further apart).

The weight of the loaded aeroplane will determine how long it takes to accelerate to that speed needed to lift off, think about your car fully loaded, full of people, full to the brim with gasoline, it's really sluggish and takes a long while to get up to speed.

So now the crew have determined from charts and graphs that they have a maximum weight that they can safely depart from that runway.

Now it is the job of the load control department to adjust the weight and distribution to be below that maximum weight. Most principal airports of the world are built to consider their environmental conditions and to allow the heaviest aircraft to depart in the worst meteorological conditions. Shorter runways with heavy loads are the ones that need to be considered carefully. Airfields in desert regions for example may have temperatures up to 50°C during the day and down below freezing at night which could make the difference of many tons of cargo weight on a Jumbo jet. High altitude airports such a Nairobi at 5327' (1624metres) runway length 1,3507' (4117metres) and La Paz Bolivia at an astonishing altitude of 13,313' (4000metres) and runway length of 13,123' have these long runways to enable aircraft to accelerate to the necessary lift off speed.

Where possible aircraft will always take off into wind. As an example, if the wind is blowing along the runway towards the aeroplane at say 20knots, (23mph), then before the aircraft starts moving it is already doing 23mph (airspeed) and 0mph groundspeed. Let's say lift off speed is 123mph (airspeed) then the aircraft in effect only needs to accelerate to 100mph (ground speed), it will of course continue after take off to accelerate to it's best climb speed.

Just prior to the lift off speed, is a very important speed that is referred to by pilots as V1 or commonly known as the take off safety speed. For all multi engine aircraft it is the speed before which, should an engine fail there is enough runway available to stop safely and after which there is enough runway available to reach lift off speed and safely climb away.

The Cruise

The higher a jet aeroplane flies the more fuel-efficient it becomes, and of course it is above the weather, however there is an optimum flight level to fly at for its weight. As fuel is used the aircraft becomes lighter and then a higher level is more efficient, which is why on a long flight you may hear the engine noise increase as the aeroplane climbs to a higher level, this may happen several times, which is perfectly normal.

Aircraft Pressurisation

We see now from the previous section why we need the aircraft to be pressurised: in order to be at an environmental pressure where there is enough oxygen pressure to breath. We can now see that there is a difference of pressure between the inside and outside of the aircraft, so at cruising altitude up to 40,000 feet there would be a differential pressure between inside and outside of around 8 psi. In order to keep the differential pressure to a workable limit, the inside of the aircraft is at a pressure equivalent to about 8000 feet altitude, where we still have plenty of oxygen.

I have been asked if it would be possible to open a door at cruising altitude, well in a word no. If you think of the size of an average airliner door, and 8lbs acting on each square inch then you may well need to be able to exert an inward force of 7 tons. Ok next question, why don't they blow out? Well they are all made as a plug type so that they become more tightly and firmly sealed as the differential pressure increases.

Ok now lets say we lose pressurisation for some reason (I'm struggling to think of one) The first thing to happen would be the oxygen masks would drop down in front of us, give it a tug to start the flow of 100% oxygen, put it on before helping anyone else. The next thing to happen would be the pilots would initiate a rapid descent down to an altitude below 10,000 feet where we can now breath normally without the need for the oxygen masks. All jet pilots practise this procedure regularly in the simulator so that if it were ever to happen to them they would be well prepared to deal with that situation. The aircraft is pressurised by air from the compressor section of the engines and regulated by outflow valves situated usually at the back of the fuselage. As air is compressed in the engines it becomes heated and this air is temperature regulated to be around a comfortable 24°C, this temperature can be adjusted up or down to different parts of the cabin. It is incredible to think that less than 1 foot or 30 cm's away on the outside of the aeroplane it is around 56° C below zero.

The Descent

The process of descent starts quite a way from the destination. Basically the aircraft becomes a glider as the engines are brought back to idle (like tick-over on your car) at the beginning of descent and not usually brought back up to power until close to the destination airfield. It's probably cheating a bit but on-board computers determine the point at which to start descent, but the pilots mostly always calculate where that point is by a simple rule of thumb. Generally I used to use the altitude in thousands of feet, so 42,000 feet would be 42 then multiply by 3 which equates to 126 nautical miles which in turn is 144 statute miles (230Kms), which in turn is roughly equal to about 30 minutes to touchdown.

During the descent air traffic control may require a slower or faster speed to sequence arriving aircraft so it may be necessary to use speed brakes which cause a little vibration (if you are sitting by a window looking at the wing you would see them come up), or hear the engines increase noise. All these noises and vibrations are perfectly normal. The landing speed will now be calculated depending upon the landing weight. The arrival procedure will be just like in chapter 7 unless you are arriving at a far flung destination without many landing aids where a visual approach would be carried out.

Jet Streams

We talked a little about winds and turbulence in chapter 6 (Weather and Turbulence).

Increasingly now we have become more aware of jet streams by watching the weather forecasts on TV. So what is a jet stream and how does it affect our flight? A jet stream is a fast moving, meandering tunnel of air, which occurs at the boundary between cold and warm air masses in the upper atmosphere around the world. The movement of the two air masses against each other and the rotation of the earth combine to give the jets their speed.

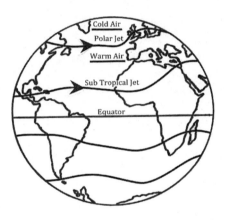

The Diagram shows west to east flow of both jet streams. The southern hemisphere is similar to the North with Polar Jet and Sub tropical jet streams. As the sun moves northwards in the summer so the Jet streams in the northern and southern hemispheres move northwards

The Polar jets are generally situated around 60° North and 60° south but for our purposes we'll only consider the northern hemisphere. The exact position varies tremendously and will move further north in the summer months and move southwards in the winter. They normally exist at around 30-39,000 feet (right in the band where we fly) and can have speeds of up to 200 MPH at the core centre of the stream.

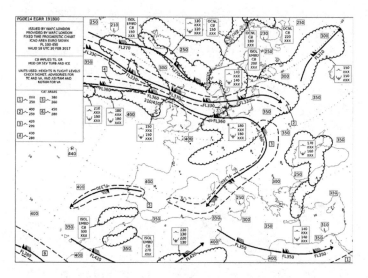

Chart courtesy of the meteorological office UK

The black lines represent the jet streams, and this chart is for February over Europe and shows a 140-knot (160 mph) jet over Scotland at 33.000 feet, and another one next to it at 36,000 feet.

The centre of the jet can be extremely smooth and most eastbound flights will try to obtain a flight level at the centre of the core, as this will reduce flight time considerably and of course save a tremendous amount of fuel. Conversely any flights going westbound will try to avoid the jet streams where possible. The jet streams meander and can turn in any direction and even break for a distance, so for flight planning purposes on long flights it is important to have the latest upper air meteorological forecasts. When on transatlantic or north pacific flights where a route has been defined it may sometimes not be possible to reroute and then one can have a bumpy ride, but generally this will be known about before the flight so a better route will have been requested.

There are two other jet streams called, the subtropical jet which is a lot weaker than the polar jet and the equatorial jet which is generally at an altitude that wouldn't be of concern around 40-45,000 feet.

Clouds

There are many different types of clouds, different shapes and sizes as we all have seen just looking up into the sky, but what is the significance to us as passengers on a flight somewhere? It would be extremely rare to fly anywhere without having at some stage to fly through clouds and sometimes they can give us a little bumpiness (not turbulence) other times we pass through them and not even know we have done.

To put this in its simplest form, air rises and in doing so it cools and the moisture within condenses to form visible moisture, ie clouds. Where there is a strong vertical current of moisture laden air, clouds can form and rise to extreme altitudes, thunderclouds or cumulonimbus as they are referred to, they have a typical anvil shape at the top. Modern weather radar gives a very good indication of where these clouds are and so enables pilots to navigate around them. Weather fronts have associated clouds and generally will herald the onset of rain.

The base of clouds can be quite low, hill fog as its name suggests can be a stratiform cloud down to the hill tops, stratus can form as a layer from lower levels in the hundreds of feet, to altostratus from anywhere between 2000 and 23,000 feet. A black looking cloud called nimbostratus generally will be a rain bearing cloud. The really high cloud called cirrus, sometimes called a mackerel sky or mares tails exist around the top of the tropopause. The fair weather clouds called cumulus generally form below 6,000 feet with a base around 2-3,000 feet. One of the really great things about taking off on a cold dank drizzly day, is when climbing up to break through the top of the stratus layer clouds into the bright sunshine, you feel one of the privileged few. Sometimes you can look down and see a fog covered countryside with hills and tall chimneys poking through the top and again be privileged to be able to feel the warmth of the sun through the cabin windows.

CLOUDS

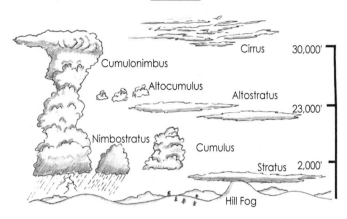

I hope the information in this chapter has helped you to gain a better understanding of some of the considerations that are taken into account before during and after a flight. Also I hope some of the misunderstandings people have about flying have been clarified. Did you know there is a generally accepted maxim that the more one understands about a subject that had given rise to anxiety, it can greatly help to diminish and eventually dispel any fears. If you do take a flight and you have any anxiety, please don't feel in any way ashamed to let the cabin staff know. They are trained to help and do everything they can to make your journey as stress free as possible.

Postscript

There are numerous books and relaxation tapes and CDs available beside this one and a good bookshop will be able to help you with obtaining them, and together with a good therapy programme you should be able to conquer your fear of flying. It is worth bearing in mind that year on year technology advances at a progressive rate and in doing so those technological advances are constantly being applied to aircraft and flight safety, commercial flying is the safest form of activity and rightly it continues to uphold that principal.

But remember just reading is not enough, you have to work at it by following the instructions, yes it could be scary at times and it would be easier to not bother and (avoid) the flight altogether, but running away isn't the answer, is it? We all know that we have had to work at anything in life to achieve our goals; nothing comes easy as they say. So by determination and perseverance and a degree of courage you will achieve that goal of being able to fly without fear. My best wishes to you all and I hope I end up sitting next to you on a flight somewhere.